P I A N O · V O C A L · G U I T A R

CHART HITS OF '95-'96

This publication is not for sale in
the E.C. and/or Australia
or New Zealand.

ISBN 0-7935-6291-0

HAL•LEONARD™
CORPORATION
7777 W. BLUEMOUND RD. P.O. BOX 13819 MILWAUKEE, WI 53213

CHART HITS OF '95-'96

ALWAYS

Words and Music by
JON BON JOVI

This Ro-me-o is bleed-ing,
pic-tures that you left be-hind are just

Well, there ain't no luck ___ in these

when I die ___ you'll be on my mind ___ and I'll love you,

al - ways.

Guitar solo - ad lib. and Fade

Repeat ad lib. and Fade

Lead vocal ad lib.

AS I LAY ME DOWN

Words and Music by
SOPHIE B. HAWKINS

BEAUTIFUL LIFE

Words and Music by JONAS BERGGREN
and ULF EKBERG

BACK FOR GOOD

Words and Music by
GARY BARLOW

BELIEVE

Words and Music by ELTON JOHN
and BERNIE TAUPIN

I be-lieve in love.

I be-lieve in love.

Repeat and Fade

BLESSED

Words and Music by ELTON JOHN
and BERNIE TAUPIN

1. Hey you,— you're a child— in my head,— you have-n't

walked yet,— your first words have yet to— be said,— but I swear

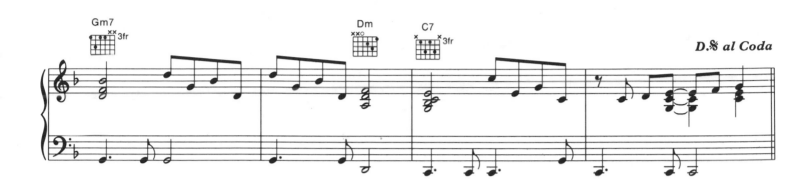

D.%. al Coda

CODA

- mise you that,___ pro - mise you that.___ You, you'll be blessed,

___ you'll have the best,___ I pro-mise you that.___ I'll pick a star from the sky,___

pull your name from a hat,____ I pro - mise you that,__ pro -

- mise you that,__ pro - mise you that,__ you'll

be_____ blessed._____

Pro -

COLORS OF THE WIND
from Walt Disney's POCAHONTAS

Music by ALAN MENKEN
Lyrics by STEPHEN SCHWARTZ

CIRCLE OF LIFE

Music by ELTON JOHN
Lyrics by TIM RICE

DIGGIN' ON YOU

Words and Music by
BABYFACE

DREAMING OF YOU

Words and Music by FRANNE GOLDE
and TOM SNOW

DO YOU SLEEP?

Words and Music by
LISA LOEB

MCA music publishing

FANTASY

Lyrics by MARIAH CAREY, TINA WEYMOUTH and CHRIS FRANTZ
Music by MARIAH CAREY, DAVE HALL, TINA WEYMOUTH,
CHRIS FRANTZ, ADRIAN BELEW and STEPHEN STANLEY

I CAN LOVE YOU LIKE THAT

Words and Music by STEVE DIAMOND,
MARIBETH DERRY and JENNIFER KIMBALL

Moderately (not too fast)

They

read you Cin-der-el-la, you hoped it would come true that
nev-er make a prom-ise I don't in-tend to keep. So,

I KNOW

Lyric by MILTON DAVIS
Music by MILTON DAVIS and WILLIAM DUVALL

I know what you're do- in', yeah, _____ yeah. I know why you
do- in', yeah, _____ yeah. I could nev- er

I'LL MAKE LOVE TO YOU

Words and Music by
BABYFACE

Close your eyes, make a wish, and blow
lax, let's go slow. I ain't

I BELIEVE

Words and Music by JEFFREY PENCE,
ELIOT SLOAN and EMOSIA

Walk blind - ly to ___ the light ___ and reach out for ___ his hand.
Vi - o - lence has spread ___ world wide and there's fam - 'lies on ___ the street.
I've been see - ing Lis - a now for a lit - tle o - ver a year.

love will find __ a way. ____

D.S. al Coda

I'LL STAND BY YOU

Words and Music by CHRISSIE HYNDE,
TOM KELLY and BILLY STEINBERG

Oh, why you look so sad, the tears are in your eyes, come on and come to me now. And don't be a-shamed to cry, let me see you through, 'cause I've seen the dark side too.

IN THE HOUSE OF STONE AND LIGHT

Words and Music by
MARTIN PAGE

O Mount Kai - las, un - cov - er me; — come
Ho - ly La - dy, show — me — my soul; — tell

— my res - to - ra - tion, wash — my bod - y clean. —
— me of — that place — where I — must sure - ly go. —

LET HER CRY

Words and Music by DARIUS CARLOS RUCKER, EVERETT DEAN FELBER,
MARK WILLIAM BRYAN and JAMES GEORGE SONEFELD

MISSING

Words and Music by BEN WATT
and TRACEY THORNE

Moderate Dance Tempo

I step off __ the train. __ I'm
Could you __ be dead? __ You

walk-ing down __ your street __ a-gain and past __ your __ door,
al-ways were __ two steps __ a-head of __ ev-'ry-one. __

but you don't live __ there an-y-more. __ It's
We'd walk be - hind __ while you would run. __ I

ONE SWEET DAY

Words and Music by MARIAH CAREY, WALTER AFANASIEFF, SHAWN STOCKMAN,
MICHAEL McCARY, NATHAN MORRIS and WANYA MORRIS

Lyrics:
Sor - ry I nev - er told ___ you all I want - ed to say. ___ And now it's too late to hold ___ you, 'cause you've flown ___ a - way, ___ so ___

NAME

Gtr. Tuning:
(1) = E   (4) = E
(2) = E   (5) = A
(3) = A   (6) = D

Words and Music by
JOHN RZEZNIK

Moderately (not too slow)

This guitar riff is played beginning on the 9th fret.

Lyrics:
Even though the moment passed me by, I
Scars are souvenirs you never lose, the
I think about you all the time, but

And I won't tell 'em your name.

Instrumental solo - ad lib.

ONLY WANNA BE WITH YOU

Words and Music by DARIUS CARLOS RUCKER, EVERETT DEAN FELBER, MARK WILLIAM BRYAN and JAMES GEORGE SONEFELD

Gtr.: Capo I

Moderately fast Rock

You and me, ___ we come from dif-f'rent worlds. ___

ROLL TO ME

Words and Music by
JUSTIN CURRIE

RUNAWAY

Words and Music by JANET JACKSON,
JAMES HARRIS III and TERRY LEWIS

Moderately slow

1. I've seen the world, been to man-y plac-es.

RUNAWAY

Words and Music by JIM CORR, SHARON CORR,
CAROLINE CORR and ANDREA CORR

SOON AS I GET HOME

Words and Music by FAITH EVANS, SEAN "PUFFY" COMBS,
CARL THOMPSON and KEVIN COTTON

Slowly, somewhat freely

THIS AIN'T A LOVE SONG

Words and Music by JON BON JOVI,
RICHIE SAMBORA and DESMOND CHILD

Slowly

I should have seen it com-ing when the ros - es died,
Ba-by, I thought you and me would stand the test of time,

should have seen the end of sum - mer ____ in your eyes.
like we got a - way with the ____ per - fect crime,

I should have lis-tened when you said "Good night." You real - ly meant good-bye. __
but we were just a leg - end in my mind. I guess that I was blind. _

wrong, yeah, I'm wrong, __ this ain't _____ a love song. Then I'm

wrong, yeah, I'm wrong, __ this ain't a love song. _____

Repeat and Fade

WHEN YOU SAY NOTHING AT ALL

Words and Music by DON SCHLITZ
and PAUL OVERSTREET

Moderately slow

It's a-maz - ing how_ you can speak right _ to my heart._
All day long _ I can hear peo - ple talk - ing out loud, _

With-out say - ing a word _
but when you_ hold me near _

D.S. al Coda

The

CODA

when you say noth-ing at all. ___

rit.

TIME

Words and Music by DARIUS CARLOS RUCKER, EVERETT DEAN FELBER,
MARK WILLIAM BRYAN and JAMES GEORGE SONEFELD

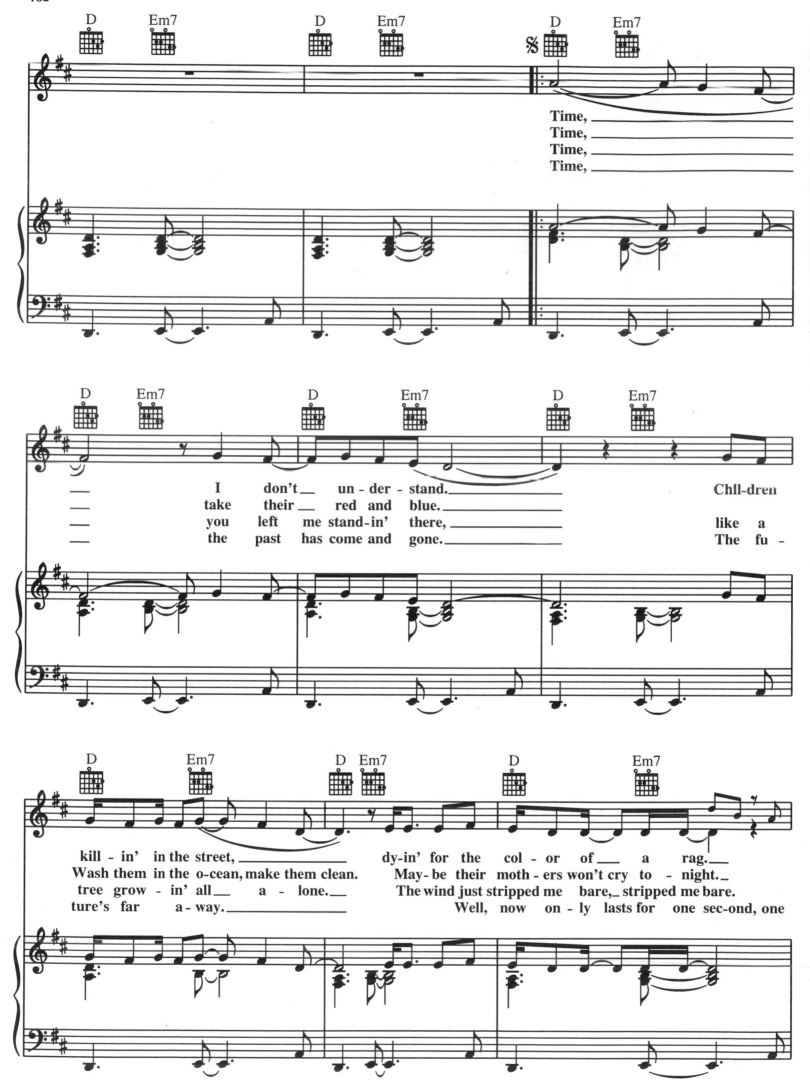

WATER RUNS DRY

Words and Music by
BABYFACE

WATERFALLS

Words and Music by MARQUEZE ETHERIDGE, LISA NICOLE LOPES,
RICO R. WADE, PAT BROWN and RAMON MURRAY

Relaxed R&B shuffle

A lone-ly moth-er gaz-ing out of her win-dow star-ing

Lit-tle pre-cious has a nat-'ral ob-ses - sion for temp-

gon - na have it your way or noth - ing at all, but I think you're

mov - ing too fast.

Repeat and Fade

Additional Lyrics

Rap: I seen a rainbow yesterday
But too many storms have come and gone
Leavin' a trace of not one God-given ray
Is it because my life is ten shades of gray
I pray all ten fade away
Seldom praise Him for the sunny days
And like His promise is true
Only my faith can undo
The many chances I blew
To bring my life to anew
Clear blue and unconditional skies
Have dried the tears from my eyes
No more lonely cries
My only bleedin' hope
Is for the folk who can't cope
Wit such an endurin' pain
That it keeps 'em in the pourin' rain
Who's to blame
For tootin' caine in your own vein
What a shame
You shoot and aim for someone else's brain
You claim the insane
And name this day in time
For fallin' prey to crime
I say the system got you victim to your own mind
Dreams are hopeless aspirations
In hopes of comin' true
Believe in yourself
The rest is up to me and you

WHEN CAN I SEE YOU

Words and Music by
BABYFACE

YOU'LL SEE

Words and Music by DAVID FOSTER
and MADONNA